OBSESSIONAL

OBSESSIONAL

Sandy McIntosh

Poetry for Performance

Marsh Hawk Press • New York • 2017

First Edition

2 4 6 8 9 7 5 3 1

Marsh Hawk Press books are published by Marsh Hawk Press, Inc.,
a not-for-profit corporation under section 501(c)3
United States Internal Revenue Code

ACKNOWLEDGEMENTS
"Obsessional" in a different form in *The After-Death History of My Mother*, Marsh
Hawk Press, 2005. "Ernesta"in a different form in *Ernesta, In the Style of the
Flamenco*, Marsh Hawk Press, 2010. "Ernesta" was read in several venues by the
author. An excerpt appears on YouTube.

Library of Congress Cataloging-in-Publication Data

Names: McIntosh, Sandy, 1947- author.
Title: Obsessional / Sandy McIntosh.
Description: New York : Marsh Hawk Press, 2017. | "Poetry for performance."
Identifiers: LCCN 2017026159 | ISBN 9780996427593 (softcover)
Classification: LCC PS3613.C54 O25 2017 | DDC 811/.6~dc23 LC record avail-
able at https://lccn.loc.gov/2017026159

Marsh Hawk Press
P. O. Box 206
East Rockaway, New York 11518-0206
www.marshhawkpress.org

CONTENTS

ERNESTA

ELEVEN CANTOS

for Susan Bailey

CHARACTER, SETTING AND STAGE

Music will watch us drown.–James Tate, "Read the Great Poets"

ERNESTA: A pianist. Dressed with a hint of the Flamenco tradition she has sported all her life.

THE TIME: Beginning of the 20th century.

THE STAGE: Ermesta sits at stage center. To her right might be an old upright piano. Above her might be an improvised screen for projections. To her left is an antique gramophone. A music stand or small lectern to her side.

IF THERE IS A PIANO: Ernesta's hands throughout the performance often seem about to touch the piano keys to illustrate the music, but hesitates and pulls them back without playing, until the penultimate scene.

GRAMAPHONE: This is a way for Ernesta to illustrate the music she mentions in her story. The turntable is always turning and Ernesta raises and places the tone arm at appropriate points on the record.

ERNESTA:

1.

¡Ay!

That old bastard Leschetitzky,

To whom I was sent to study in 1885

Pushed me out disdainfully

(After I'd rejected him) onto

Clara Wieck, relic of the dead composer,

Robert Schumann,

At Frankfurt am Main,

And mistress (I didn't know at the time)

Of that fellow Brahms.

She was, I thought,

Not a bad pianist,

And she performed for me

The last sonata of Beethoven.

Superlative, the music. Like you,

I was moved to weeping.

But she took my tears

For love of her

And left the bench

To mount my lap.

"I knew you had a soul," she declared.

"I knew I could inspire it."

Saying which, she began to rub

My costume.
What could I do? I was sixteen,
She perhaps forty—altogether ancient
And unattractive, you'll agree.
But it is our duty to realize our talents.
And so, I yielded to her pleasure
With enthusiasm, and at length.

"You must wear your costume
        On stage, at receptions," Wieck instructed,
                Directing my career.
"The music can never be enough
        For the bored husband in attendance,
                Or the jaded wife. You must distract them
From the incomprehensible,
        Let them pass the time
                Avec plaisir."

She was here
        Referring to my costume—
                A Flamenco dancer's,
Something my mother had sent
        From home—I could not imagine why.

"It's a handy prop," Wieck explained.
        "The vest with satin and gold ruffles—
                So heroic—
And the revealing trousers, also,

10

So feminine."

¡Ay! ¡Ay! ¡Ay!

2.

So, onto the stage she thrust me,

    Arranging concerts

        In little theaters in great cities,

Always in the shadow of her true lover,

    The bumptious Brahms.

We were oddly twined, Brahms and I.

    He overwhelming the Grosser Musikvereinssaal in

Vienna

        While I, the plodding dray-horse,

Through Malagueñas, Grana'nas, Media Grana'nas,

    And other tedious transcriptions

[Grammaphone plays "Mexican Hat Dance"]

    Of Spanish dance music

For the Ladies' Tea Society,

    Or some such,

        Located somewhere

            Near the wharf.

In his splendid dressing rooms

    Brahms received the King and Queen.

        I, in my turn,

Attended the

    the Ladies in Waiting,

Waiting for me,
In my backstage
Hole in the wall.

"You are, after all, the beginner.
There is a price to pay for advancement.
Pay it, grin and be happy," ordered Wieck.
¡Ay! ¡Ay! ¡Ay!

3.
It was, I must say, a lovely,
Lucrative time. Lachrymose, the
Germans for music, crying at
Each arabesque, every waltz, the

Ushers running the aisles with lace
Handkerchiefs for the ladies. They
Cried in the streets for a pop-
ular tune.

And, God help us, When a
Fashionable composer died!
Old Glück's funeral—four months long!
Multitudes of musicians in
His memory. Accompanists
to the country's wistful, obliv-
ious... dreaming....

And I also dreamed deeply
On my concert stage,
Fascinated spectator
To imaginative scenes unfolding
In my mind as I played:
Elaborated image upon image.
And, over years,
My visions joined by dream actors
Who never failed to amuse.
I never asked, "Where am I?"
So certain was I of my strengths.

Old Beethoven in his time
Laughed at his audience
As, by mere whim,
He played to make them weep,
or whimpering silent—
Or, who knows? Feint dead away.

I, too, made listeners quake,
But I loved them (unlike him)
And only wanted them
To witness what I saw—
Those ecstatic things.
And, naturally,
They did see,
And honored me
With applause

Joyful noise,
Duly noted by
Music critics.
"Señora Ernesta Pleases."
¡Ay! ¡Ay! ¡Ay!

4.
I pleased them—
I pleased myself—
In every European country,
Yet Wieck kept me
In Flamenco costume,
And touring everywhere but Spain
(Where they preferred
German pianists
In lugubrious
lederhosen).

All went well.
I played a wider repertoire
Dropping stale Spanish ditties
For music of weight,
Of darker dreaming,
Yet always pleasing my audience,

With novelties
As finale.
My special piano

[Grammaphone plays mad piano music]

Made by mad

Clement of New York.

At my whim it would

Chirp like a bird, croak like a frog,

Boom like a thunderclap, howl

Like a dog in heat, shriek

Like a parrot, or

Emit rude sounds of

The water closet.

But then

(It was somewhere eastward, I think,

In the Ottoman Empire),

Something went wrong:

On stage, playing dream music

The audience with me

(I could hear them swaying,

Moaning

In their seats),

As I brought the music

To its graceful end,

(So I thought),

I found myself

Not at the piano,

But in the wings,

In my street costume

About to leave the theatre.

[stage light out. Voice from wings:]

What had happened?
"You walked out before finishing, Mademoiselle,"
Said the stage manager,
Perplexed.
The audience behind us
Restive, uncertain.

[stage light on:]

What had happened?

I'd been playing
Robert Schumann's "The Poet Speaks",
[Grammaphone plays: "The Poet Speaks"]

Its lovely grace, its sadness.
I alone on the empty stage,
In dreaming. As usual,
The music done, I bowed,
Retired in modest dignity,
A caress to the souls
Of each listener.
But this night
I had not
Awoken from the dream.
(That must be the answer, I surmised.
I'd remained in the music

16

Even leaving the stage
And almost into the street.)

5.
Next night:
Again it happened.
Am I mad?

I consulted Wieck.
She looked at me sadly,
Concerned.

"This is what happened to Robert,"
Her husband, the dead Schumann.
"He wandering away
into his dream,
never returning."

(I'd heard Schumann had died in Bedlam.)

[Ominous, loud-she's making her point]

"It's a conceit, affectation, indulgence
To pretend music has pictures,
Has a story to tell.
Robert knew, in truth,
That music is only music,
Though that knowledge
Gained him nothing."

[innocent:]

> For my part,
> I had no idea what she meant.
> Music, of course, had stories
> And pictures, to pull
> Us away
> From quotidian quarrelsomeness,
> Waking-life vexation.

[as Wieck: intense]

> "Music," she continued,
> "Is a wild beast.
> She must be
> controlled,
> caged
> Else she turn upon you
> Destroying all."

> Unbelieving, I
> Shook my head
> Not speaking.

> "You need to see.
> I'll show you," she declared,
> And took me
> To Byreuth, to vulgar Wagner's operas,
> > *Der Ring des Nibelungen.* The Ride of the Valkyries!

[Grammaphone plays Wagner: "Ride of the Valkyries"]

The horror of them!
¡Ay! ¡Ay! ¡Ay!
Through their music
I saw what Wagner saw:
Shades of the monumental:
Males and females towering above mountains,
Lumbering over the earth,
Lathering bloody ancient ritual,
Never intended for
Modern times.

"To loosen grasping grip
On him, Robert
recklessly wrote
Music without program,
Without picture,
But picaresque withal, you see,
And touching, too:
'The Poet Speaks'

[Grammaphone plays "The Poet Speaks" cont.]

His first attempt.
To break the curse—no pictures
At all! Or so he thought.
"It turned out
To be the worse for him,

Losing his way to the music's end
Without the markers, the maps.
The pictures.
And, at last,
He was lost.
Alack."

Lest I, too, lose my way,
She told me
I must avoid all music with programs,
With stories, damn pictures
Able to lead me to
Unknowable dungeons
Of darkness in dream.

6.
Fear and caution
Gathered me in,
Nourishing my performance
With hungry diet
Of the safe
And acceptable
"You cannot afford," said Wieck,
"To disgrace yourself upon the stage.
Not even once!"

So, it was back to the safety
Of Malagueñas, Grana'nas, Media Grana'nas,

And other tedious transcriptions
Of Spanish dance music.

[Grammaphone plays "Mexican Hat Dance" repeat]

Twice I attempted to break free,
Challenging the forbidden
"The Poet Speaks,"
The first time with mild success,
But the second
With terror,
Finding myself in the stalls,
Applauding wildly,
While the audience stared
At the empty stage.

From then, I resolved to ply
The narrow road
Without imagination.

I was already forty
And should have been
At my zenith.
But still I performed
In Flamenco costume,
Though certain sure
I'd outgrown it
Long before.
Humiliation shared residency

With what triumph
I achieved.

Worse,
My modest sensation and fame
Had competitors.
Two especially (I won't mention names)
Attempted to crowd me
From the stage.
One toured with burros
That wandered about
Diverting audience attention.
Another boasted
Masked dancers
In silent pantomime.
Both, of course,
Imitated my costume,
But elaborated
Upon it:
One by smoldering phosphorous flairs,
The other by transportable
Electric lights.

7.
They were nothing,
No threat to me,
Like the real threat
Of Enrique

Granados.
He, a likeable man,
A genuine Spaniard,
Wore no special costume
When performing—instead
In mufti—and playing
His own compositions,
Originals,
That left the sting of lemon
On your tongue,
And the red Sahara dust
Of the leveche
On your tongue,
And the yawning
In coolness
Of the afternoon veranda.
Tro-pi-cal is what he was,
And boon
To frigid European winter.

[Grammaphone plays Granados: "Spanish Dance #1"]

He was my enemy,
Though I liked him
Well enough,
And sympathized silently
His suffering
Hallucinations
And terrible stage fright.

I offered my council,
Telling him: "Don't worry.
Just go out there. You'll think
Of something."
And, against my true hope,
He did, always.

I copied his improvisations,
Claiming them for my own.
(I, by then,
So frightened
By imagination's wildness
That I could do
Little else.)

He, in turn,
Loved me,
Questioning me about life
And travel—something he feared
Greatly.
Then (it was 1913 or 1914)
His composition Goyescas found
International success,
And he received an invitation
From America,
To concertize
For the President.
Impossibly nervous,

He asked would I go with him,
Discretely, of course.
He had certain nightmares
While playing his piano....
He'd pay my way
I to stay with him
For companionship,
No personal intrigue,
Help him
Understand the New World.
He'd pay my way.

He'd pay my way.
It would be the retainer
And the retained.
But, why not?

I could see very well
The end of Germany,
The sentimental music
Fueling visions
Of majestic ascendancy.
Germany
Apex of Europe—
Her composers
Told her so.
Why not go with the boy?
But his dreadful foreshadowing:

"I play my music
And dream of the ship
Torpedoed," he confessed.
"The seawater
In my nose,
Choking me, filling
My lungs.
I know this to be
Hallucination,
But come with me.
At least keep my mind
From the bottom
Of the sea."

Hallucinations
They were,
So much like my own,
But, for him,
Not far off the mark:

The warring powers
With deadly sea weapons:
Sinking ships.
Our daily news.

8.
Consulted I with Clara Wieck.
        She (one hundred years old

If a day by now)
Was doyenne of composers,
Beloved of the powerful.
She advised:
"Go. There is nothing
For you here."

She arranged passage
From France
On the Mirabelle,
A Spanish freighter.
"My friends inform me
That Spanish ships
May pass our blockade
Unharmed. It is
The English ships
That must capsize."

9.
At the dock
Granados waited
Nervous, pacing.

'So glad to see you!'
Clutching the hem of my mantón.
"I thought you would never come.
The most awful dream!
I dreamed it

Last afternoon
At the salon
At which I played."

"Ah," I tried to reassure him.
"It was only a dream.
Music does that
To us all.
"Mirabelle is
A solid ship. A Spanish ship.
We will feel
At home."

"The dream so vivid!"
Stammered he. "The ocean
Broke through the walls!
I? Swept away!
Then you?
Sitting in a lifeboat.
You waved your fan. 'Bon voyage!'
Paddling away."

He began to cry;
I patted his shoulder.

The Mirabelle sounded
Her great horn. Granados
Refused to board.

"I cannot travel

    On this ship,"

        Declared he

            With finality.

I reasoned:

    "All our luggage—your beautiful piano

      All are aboard!"

"No, no. You sail,"

    Said he, eyes lolling.

        "I'll take the next ship.

Which one? Ah!

    The Exeter sails Friday.

        I'll take the Exeter,

            A good British ship."

"No!" I cried,

    But he not listening.

        I could have told him

British ships

    Would be torpedoed.

        But, no. I did not.

A terrible sin of omission?

    Or was it the tact

      Of a lady?

"Next Wednesday," said he

With wild grin.
    "We meet in New York
        Next Wednesday!"

Arrived in New York,
    The news report said
        The Exeter had been sunk
Only a few miles
    From Le Havre.
        Survivors,
            There were none.

10.
In short,
Granados dead,
I was offered
His place, playing
For the American president
As I had suspected
I might.
I had taken the precaution
Of registering
In my own name
All his original compositions,
His wonderful piano! Its
Rosewood cover!

And so I became established
Unchallenged, respected
The greatest interpreter
Of the works
Of Enrique Granados
(Which I, at times
Of convenience to me,
Called my own
Compositions).

For several years, at least
My longevity in the public eye,
Enhanced via
Old Leschetitzky,
Who, now arrived in New York,
A sentimental place
In his halting heart,
Coaxed me to play
For the mechanical piano
Granados' music,
To make piano rolls
For the wide appreciation
Of music-loving
But illiterate
Public.

Thus when nightmares on stage
Returned,

(Young Granados
In the sea, willing water
To solidify for handhold,
Failing, drowning,)
I could tease tunes
Safely
From the player piano
With pumping pedestrian feet,
Staying trembling,
Haunted hands.

When I play
For my public now
I play for safety—no silly
Pictures in my head
To preoccupy me,
Only the plodding
Scales, chords, the arpeggios
Of the novice—
At adventurous times,
The exercises of Hannon,
And Clementi—
That in lesser hands
Might seem ridiculous,
Elementary. But genius
Will out!

[End "Spanish Dance"
Grammaphone plays scratchy static background.
If there is a piano on stage, Ernesta strikes the keys violently
playing a scale, arpeggio, or other elementary piano exercise as if
performing the climatic movement of a masterpiece.]

11.

And I am never reckless!

My arms and torso

I do not wave about

Like a puto!

No more

Wild musical

dreams!

¡Ay! ¡Ay! Ay!

And after my concerts

I read the newspaper

And it is always:

"Señora Ernesta Pleases."

She is a wild animal,   this music,

She must be   controlled,

Caged   else she turn upon you

Destroying all.

Arrogant armies   stamping feet across

Continents   Inspired, each one,

By some   affected anthem

Dribbling sentiment,   some musical monstrosity
Imaginary righteousness.   What better exemplar
Of menace   and disgrace?

If I may present you a proverb
Of my own invention:
"Music ," I will caution you.
"Music will watch us drown."
¡Ay! ¡Ay! Ay!

I applaud myself: ¡Olé!

[Curtain]

OBSESSIONAL

ELEVEN CANTOS

STAGE, NARRATOR, SHADOW, LIGHTING

STAGE: Bare stage except for a lectern center stage a chair stage left of it, and a tall white screen in the background upon which a 10 foot high black shadow (silhouette) is projected. Although the shadow appears to be the **NARRATOR's**, it is actually **MAX's**. The shadow changes shape as directed.

LIGHTING: soft, nondescript at rise. When **NARRATOR** begins to speak, spotlight finds him.

At rise, we see the **NARRATOR** sitting in the chair next to the lectern, facing the audience.

NARRATOR:

(Rises, stands behind the lectern. Shuffles papers, getting organized. Looks up at audience. Spot on NARRATOR. MAX's shadow, contorted, is thrown upon the screen.)

1.

I open the door

and there's the famous poet,
Max, dancing about:
black hair, beard, fierce horse'
eyes, chanting loudly
with the radio:

"Move bitch, get
out da way.
Get out da way bitch, get out da way..."

I've heard about him,
of course, read his work.

This evening, our first together
as roommates,
grad students
at a summer course
at this ancient university:
I'm speechless.
"I'll compromise," he says

studying my face.
"I'll only play it
on my side of the room. How's that?"

"Ludicrous," I mutter.

"Oh, you know the artist?
Ludacris?"

Before I answer
he's turned up the volume:

"Move bitch, get out da way.
Get out da way bitch, get out da way..."

2.

[Lights dim—it's a dorm party.]

A first night's
party—red wine,
paper cups,
cheese cubes.

Max and I huddling
behind hands, speculating
on others: "You see
him?" whispers Max. "Eyeballs
swiveling like that? Irish,

for sure. Hears the inner voices.
Doubtlessly homicidal."

I, liking this game, whisper back:
"That woman: Long black
hair, lacey dress. She keeps knives
in that blouse,
I'll bet."

"Not knives," says Max. "But sharp
enough. It's Margarita.
Watch out."

And Margarita turns as if
she'd heard; strides over:
"You two: Spanish
aunts, gossiping
behind fans. Be ashamed!"

Max giggles; tangos
fiendish steps.
I, reddened,
allege one strangled
"Olé!"

3.

[Shadow: Max in profile, holding open book]

"This is how I get the girls," Max whispers,
about to read
his poetry.
"Yes," I whisper back.
"I'd like to see you do that."

I really would, since Max's poetry
is sentimental horseshit
and nobody should fall for it.

Yet, when he begins to read,
I watch the girls look up with interest
at his story of brothers
in their little town—how sad when one disappears
in autumn, in the lake, under a running tide,
at sunset.

Others are taken
by his story of first love—her
parting words to him—heartbreaking and yet
with delicious irony,
and hilarious because of it ...

... and so on he reads,
and on,

until, I swear, every woman in the room
is taken, and,

                                         in truth, I may be a little
taken,
myself.

When he's done, the girls collect around,
some teary eyed with wistful
smiles, but all with pens
for him to sign
the books he's thoughtfully brought
to sell. ("Always carry your books,"
he sotto voce instructs. "You never know when
your market will get hot.")
To each girl he whispers something,
in answer to her praise. I can't quite
make out what he says,
but he says it with sincerity.
("Oh yes," he instructs
afterwards. "You must learn
to do
'sincere'
really, really well.")

4.

[Shadow: Max sitting quietly.]

My turn upon
the stage. And I've got
something

that'll hold their attention—
like Max, something
that'll get the girls.
"This," I begin,
"is a story of the hijacking
of English poetry
in the year 1559!
Of forgery, duplicity,
prosody!"

I pause. This
is going to be good.

It's 1559. Martyrs' fires burn
in England—
a time of political correctness
and innovation, as well.
Commerce with Europe
brings contact with Continental
literature—judged superior
to the home-grown kind.

In London, printer
Richard Tottel sees a market
among the elite, educated public
for the best new poetry
England has lately produced.
The manuscripts circulating privately

in courts could rival, if printed, anything
by Italians or French, to show
foreigners England is good—
better—than them at
their own game.

Tottel hires Nicholas Grimald,
illustrious Cambridge scholar,
translator. They collect,
carefully edit 271 poems,
mostly by Sir Francis Wyatt,
Henry Howard, Earl of Surrey,

as well by "divers
other."

The first edition,
called *Songs and Sonnets*,
sells out in weeks.
In the next months
Tottel reprints
seven times, editing, rearranging,
getting sloppier,
withal,
each edition selling out.

Meanwhile,
imitators abound:

The Paradyse of Daynte Devises, A Handefull
of Pleasant Delites, Gorgious
Gallery of Gallant Inventions,
A Mirror for Magistrates...

Songs and Sonnets is famous
for one hundred years, credited
with establishing English poetry,
especially the sonnet, the primacy of the iamb,
the patent English schema. Even Shakespeare
has Bottom lament: "I had rather than forty shillings
I had my book
of *Songs and Sonnets* here."

But there is mystery, too.
Modern scholars discover
the poems of Wyatt and Surrey
in their authors' hands
are not the same as printed
by Tottel.
Of Wyatt's "Satires," John Thompson
(*The Founding of English Metre,*
New York: Columbia University Press, 1966) writes:
"The Satires as printed by Tottle are not
Wyatt's Satires. The metrical principle
is quite different from Wyatt's; the true difference
cannot be tabulated statistically."
A.K Foxwell (*The Poems of Sir Thomas Wiat,*

London: Russel and Russel, 1964) takes it further:

"I went to the MSS. in 1906, and compared the variants with those in the author's own text... Wiat's individual characteristics were obliterated... It is evident, then, that Tottel... adopted a style of verse contrary to Wiat's method...."

"Why?" I ask rhetorically.
And answer
in Foxwell's words:
"'...to suit the views of a later
generation.'"

I pause, having
made my point. But Max
demands:

[Shadow: Max is standing, hands on hips]

"So what? So what does this prove? So what if this printer fellow cleans up primitive verse, yielding us great poetry, glory of English Lit! What's wrong with that?"

"That's all true," I say.
"But here's another way
to see: Would English poetry
have evolved in unexpected ways,
with more likeness
to its forbears—yes, Chaucer

and Langland, and even
Beowulf—poetry
more akin to the Beowulf poet shouting:
"Hwaeth! Listen up!" to his cyn—
a community event—something
for "the people," not only "the public"
(as Tottel defines),
if Grimald and friends
kept greedy hands
off genuine
merchandise?"

"I don't believe it," says Max.

"Don't you see?"
I plead,
"Don't you see that Tottel snatched
real English poetry, replacing
it with counterfeit?
Verse that sounds like nothing
anyone ever
spontaneously said?"

Silence.

I try again:
"All this time
we've seen it one way: the glorious

increase of poetry
over four hundred years."
(Here I begin to gesture
compulsively.)
"But, if you have it
the other way,
what we've got is tragedy,
forgery!"

Silence.

What I really want to do
is leap about furiously,
like the obsessed grad student I am,
to scream:
TOTTEL AND HIS HENCHMEN MUST BE ARRESTED!
MUST BE TAKEN TO THE PLACE OF DARKNESS
TO BE HANGED UNTIL
THEY ARE DEAD!
But there are limits,
and so I retreat myself
into silence.

The session over,
I'm the only one left.

5.
Later, alone with Max

I try again:
I wanted to read a poem
that I would understand. Though
I hated them all:

Among the worst
the pedestrian Longfellow:
"Evangeline" drilled by rote in school,
(Though the 'Druids of eld, with voices sad and prophetic,'
standing 'like harpers hoar, with beards that rest on their
bosoms'
amused sixth graders.)

Or murderous "Invictus"
            ('Out of the night that covers me,
            Black as the Pit from pole to pole,
            I thank whatever gods may be
            For my unconquerable soul.')
Also by rote.

And then grim Victorian tabloid poetry:
('Oh, Heaven! It was a frightful and pitiful sight to see
Seven bodies charred of the Jarvis family;
And Mrs. Jarvis was found with her child,
and both carbonized,
And as the searchers gazed thereon they were surprised.')

And the magnificent, flatulent

'Ode on the Mammoth Cheese, Weighing over 7,000
pounds':
('We have seen thee, queen of cheese,
Lying quietly at your ease,
Gently fanned by evening breeze,
Thy fair form no flies dare seize.'

Why was I the only one laughing?)

"Ho hum," yawns Max.

"And worst of all, twisting
plainspoken psalm
into tortured syntax,
(i.e. 'The Lord to me a shepherd is
Want therefore shall not I?')"

"Are you telling me
these bastardized things
are great English poems?"

"No," I retort. "But they
are the children of Tottel,
bastards nonetheless,
and we must vouchsafe
them our attention,
or what's
an English department

for?
"In any case, these things pained me."

"I can see how they would," says Max.

"Pained me,
until a friend showed
something."

"Did he, indeed?" arched brow Max.
"Was it Wordsworth:
('Give me your tool, to him I said.')
It wasn't Wordsworth, was it?"

I sputtering:
"I meant, a poem
he'd written himself,
in a language we spoke,
and not in artificial
mouthfuls that no one
ever
spontaneously
said.
And about
important things..."

"Ah," says Max. "And what meaning
did this poem hold

for you?"
I looked up,
 anywhere for the words:
"...That it was modern English,
unadorned
with obvious figures.
Yet it was to my hearing something.
Something..."

"Yes," says Max quietly. "Magic."

He understands at last, I think.
But then:

"I understand," he said
It is your
argument I don't
believe ."

6.

[Shadow: Max wearing a straw hat, like a barker]

"We'll put on a talent show,"

Max announces. It's
nearly end of summer
and school.

"Don't worry," he reassures.
"I'll arrange everything."
He sets about
recruiting class clown,
Dickie Needles, who,
known to Max only,
plays classical violin.

"When you come on,"
Max instructs,
"wear this old bathrobe.
Everyone'll think you're clowning.
Then give'em Brahms."

Max conscripts Argol, silent
the whole term, author
of a so-far incomprehensible
dissertation: "Otiose Warts."
He's discovered
Argol can recite
from memory
the complete dialogue
from the '70s disaster movie,
The Towering Inferno.
The catch is: Argol
won't introduce scenes, won't
change voice as
different characters speak,

simply recites
and recites

until stopped.

Next Max reels in
Yuki, who owns
a kimono and
a koto, six feet long
that she offers to play.

Then steely Margarita.
Large, muscular, she
announces she'll perform
graceful interpretive dances
to Yuki's playing.

"Well, she plays piano, too," Max
confides, almost an apology.
"I'll have her do
something with me
at the end."

"And what is it
you're planning to do
at the end?" I ask, suspicious.

Max, mysterious, "Perhaps

I'll sing a little."
(And
I can already hear it
in my head
"Move bitch, get
out da way.
Get out da way bitch, get out da way..."

That'll give the audience
something to think about, I warrant.)

7.

Comes show night:
wine jugs, cheese cubes
paper cups.
Everyone's pleased, eating,
drinking.

Max appears. Theatrical
bow. "Ladies and gentlemen..."

Dickie Needles,
nervous, bathrobe
flapping, arms
akimbo. We
giggle at the clowning

sure to come.
Out flourishes the violin
and his serious
music, so unexpected,
mesmerizing.

Genuine applause
when Dickie's done.

Next comes Argol Karvarkian.
Who is this
anonymous man?
Argol silent, brick-like
before us,
opens mouth,
begins....
the loudest human tone
I've ever...!
Crashing tank tread! As if
a film-looped army
endlessly
invades us.

Five, ten, fifteen
minutes of this.
I cut my eyes
and catch Max's
sadistic smirk.

Finally, Max
breaks in; shoos
Argol.

Yuki, kimonoed,
appears, koto carted
by massive Margarita. Yuki sits,
plucks strings with
plectra. Quiet sounds,
"Haru no Umi (The Sea
in Spring)."
Margarita is hard-
pressed to dance barefoot
without crushing notes
like vatted grapes. At last,
she withdraws into shadow,
as Yuki plays on to
strummed, wistful ending.

Then it's time for Max.
The audience quiet,
anticipating, clueless.
But I can't wait
to watch Max
ruin himself.

Which, of course, he doesn't.

Margarita at the keyboard
of the baby grand.
Max sprawling across
its top, crossed legs. Quietly,
as if the cafeteria lights
had gone down, as if
cafe candles were flickering.
He tells us:

"My mother
always wanted to sing
in nightclubs, with
big bands. But
she stayed home, raising us kids.
Even so, when Dad worked
the late shift, she would
sing to us."

On cue, Margarita begins
to play.

"I'm going to sing
my mother's songs."

In naive, untrained voice—
not tenor, nor baritone—
somewhere out of spectrum,

Max begins "The
Man I Love."

Some day he'll come along, the man
I love./ And he'll be big and strong, the man I
love...

He charms us, damn it.
Damn nit. Charms us
from the start! It's a torch song.
Max pretends
no skill, doesn't clown.
It's his vulnerable voice, childlike,
forever trusting mother,
that of a little boy three or
forty years old.

What can we do but cheer?
We're all happily
drunk by now, so
what the hell..

Before his
final song, some of us begin
to weep.

I begin to weep.

("It's all timing," Max
confides later. "A fart
is high art
when you cut it right.")

8.

[Shadow: Max is seated.]

I'm back

in the stacks,
worrying Tottle's
in my teeth
like a dog.

Why won't Max
believe?

"You've got to make
the case
for forgery, if that's
what you allege."

"And how am I
supposed to do
that?"
"Motive," declares Max.
"Find the motive

for it."

Start, then, with Tottel, the man:

"Richard Tottel (or Tothill)," writes Hyder Edward Rollins
(*Tottel's Miscellany*. Cambridge: Harvard University Press,
1966,) "born at Exeter about 1530... printer of distinction...
charter member of the Stationer's Company (under-warden
in 1561)"—blahdy-blahdy-blahdy—began about 1550, at the
sign of The Hand and the Star in Fleet Street. Prints law
books, mostly, Greek and Roman translations. Some minor
poetry: Tusser's rhymes on husbandry and huswifry, the
works of Sir Thomas More. Oh here: Cicero's *De Officiis*
translated by Nicholas Grimald, who later turns up as chief
editor of the *Miscellany*.

I read on
and on,

still no motive
for forgery. But
I'm after
this dude, Grimald.

Here's a mystery:

Forty poems of Grimald printed in the first edition of *Tottel's*. Eight weeks later, surpassing success, with Grimald
responsible, and a second edition appears, sells out imme-

diately. Yet, inside, only nine Grimald poems remain, and Grimald's name excised altogether. Why this messing with patent success? Why this alteration?

"Today the name of Nicholas Grimald is almost unknown," writes L. R. Merrill (*The Life and Poems of Nicholas Grimald.* New Haven: Yale University Press, 1925.) Yet his contemporaries regard him as foremost Cambridge alumnus, great English scholar, playwright, translator, teacher, preacher (chaplain to martyred Bishop Ridley) and so on. "One wonders why it is," asks Merrill, "that a man so highly rated is now quite forgotten?"

Interesting Grimald:

His father a promoter—that is, an extorter of money from the wealthy on behalf of the king. (Executed for this by a later king, although a devoted husband and kind father, according to Grimald.) At Christ Church Grimald sees published his play, *Christus Redivivus—The Resurrection of Christ.* And many times later, performed, often in Germany, where it is used as original text of Oberammergau's anti-Semitic *Passion* play, held every ten years in thanksgiving for deliverance from the Black Death. He translates Cicero's *Octavium de Republica,* Virgil's *Georgics,* and more. Then, interestingly, experiments with poetry in English applying Greek metrics, dactylic hexameter. Much technical success, to be sure, but unpleasant to the ear.

But he persists, eventually bringing the poems of Wyatt and Surrey to Tottel. Perhaps he models his own verse on Wyatt's, though we know he rewrites his betters, and, as coupde-maître, awards himself the lion's share of Tottel's pages.

Unsavory Grimald:

Ecclesiastical timeserver, shifting from Catholic to Protestant in the political wind, recanting secretly, betraying friends, "as," writes Merrill, "was necessary to save his life." His friends, hanged or burned—his, hardly the life of pure scholarship, though not unknown to the English department. The Bodleian Library holds a poem of Duke Humphrey's, Grimald's contemporary, a *Carmen in Laudem Grimmoaldi*, a song of praise, which concludes: "Since you do all things with a desire for transitory praise,/ May the gods give you praise, but brief praise, O Grimald."

Grimald rewrites the poetry in Tottel's, but why? To suit the taste of the day? No, because his rewriting establishes that taste in the first place. Because he had studied European poetic forms, judged them superior, wished to bring them to the English line? Yes. But is it forgery?

And why do I pursue this
doggedly? I ask
at day's end, at the end

of the day
I must be insane.

9.

[Shadow: Max wearing a straw hat, like a barker]

This is it

a blank night,
a break
before nervous
sessions commence,
defending our theses.

Max, heady
with triumph, announces
that tonight, in the rec. room,
he'll invent
for our amusement
the Café Casablanca.
"I'll find tablecloths. We'll
have menus. We'll serve
coffee, tea, wine. Pastry!
A real boulevard cafe!"

Everyone's thrilled,
of course. Me too. I want to help.

Max is harsh: "Why
do you always want to collaborate?
This is my party. I'm not going to let you
take credit. You're the competition,
don't you know that?"

Rejected and flattered,
both at once.

***

[Shadow: Max wearing a long coat with tails]

Eight-thirty that night:
I walk my date
Yuki
down the dorm stairs.
Max at the door,
suit and tie,
hair neat. "Welcome," he,
unctuous, greets us.
"Shall I show you
our best table for two?"

The room dusky,
flickering candles.
brutal cinder block decorated
with streamers. Each rickety table
disguised with gift paper.

"Your server," he says
"will be with you shortly."
Max is our smiling,
gracious host.

The party under way,
we are loud, celebratory,
dancing to the boom-box
Max has found.

Then, at midnight
I see Max alone,
sipping wine. "Congratulations,"
I tell him. "You've got everyone
playing a part
in your fantasy
cafe."

Max, annoyed, dismissive:
"It needs only a good idea to get them started. These people
love to role-play. That's what they've been doing since they
got here: playing the serious student role. Now, I've given
them something else to play at. They're very happy."

"Aren't you unfair?.
It's not play-acting. After all,
we are students."
Max looks at me now:

"Don't you see? It's a cover. Half these people came looking for a man, for a woman, for validation of their lives from people superior to themselves."

"What role am I playing, then?"

A pause. "You pretend," he says "to be the young apprentice. That learning for the sake of learning is a sacred, mystical quest. You act woolly-headed, confused, but you know more than you let on. You're really watching everything with a sober eye. And you're angry with me right now because I've unmasked you!"

Well, I was angry. So what?
But unmasked? I don't think so.

"Have it your way," shrugs Max. "You're deluding yourself, just like the other bozos. You think you're knights on a holy crusade. Actually, you're only the Don Quixote-types, inflating ego-needs with fantasy. You think it's the Moors attacking across the Spanish plains, but it's just a flock of sheep. That's why you all walk around bumping into each other. Your eyes are on the prize, but the prize is a mirage!"

Furious now, because I love this graduate study, my fellow students, I recall to Max the scene in *Don Quixote* wherein the innkeeper invites the insane old man to stay so he can laugh at him and have his guests laugh at him.

"Yes," Max says, "I remember."
Then, finally triumphant, I want to know:
"Why is it you innkeepers, you reality-grounded cafe owners,
why is it you get so much pleasure from torturing us poor
lunatics?"

Max is stunned, but only
a moment. And I'm gratified.
He slaps tabletop with palm. "Bravo!"
he laughs. "Touché! You got me!
I didn't think
you had it in you!"

I, relieved, flushed with gratitude,
take the hand he's offered. My anger
fizzled, he's
conceded the point.

I accept
his validation.

10.

[Shadow: Max wearing a mortor board and gown: an academic]

"I can help you," says Max.

We're allowed one
peer on our dissertation

panel. Now feeeling
on equal footing, I
invite Max onto
mine.

"I'll coach you, get
your act into shape."

We review everything I've pursued
this summer.

Max considers:
"Maybe you've found the motivation for fraud. Grimald
wants his own poems published, but nobody likes him
much. So, he does the hard work of the anthologist, puts
together something irresistible, and then gets a free ride on
Wyatt's coattails. That's his hidden agenda. "Hmm," Max
concludes. "I think it will play."

I think it does,
if somewhat.

Professors
quiet throughout
my presentation. At the end,
silence. Now,
this is the moment,
Max should jump in,

guide the proceedings,
validate my work,
concentrate
the judges' minds.

And Max does seize
that moment but only to say:
"No.
No. I just don't
believe it. He
hasn't made his
case." A sly,
smile in my direction:
"I must
vote
it down."

***

Afterwards, I
ask why? Why
this bastardly
betrayal?

"You are the
competition," he answers.
"What else did you expect?
But I already told you that,

didn't I?"

11.
"It seems strange," writes
Professor Thompson (op. cit.) "that Tottel's *Miscellany* should
rise like a wall separating poets in Tudor England."

For instance, Wyatt in his own hand: "It was no dreme: I
lay brode waking." But then revised by Grimald: "It was no
dreame: for I lay broade awaking." A subtle change,
but the line is regularized.

It felt like no dream:
I'm walking
the Tudor alleys.
A man, hurrying,
at me, his
face in my face.

[Shadow: Max jumps from his chair]

"Yo," quoth he. "Bitch.
Move."
It's Nick
Grimald—tall, thin,
eyes of a wild horse, black hair
flapping in wind.
"You got me!" he shouts.
"I didn't think

you had it in you. But
you got me."
"What?" I ask, trying
to wake up.

"But you blundered importantly.
I didn't become master of form
to imitate lesser others.
First my poems—unprecedented
in our language,
and made at great expense (witness
dead friends, milord Bishop
Ridley). Then to showcase,
I worked flawed, ratty,
rattling-on-floppy feet
rhymes of others—reformed them,
raised them up,
made them holy
or wholly imitations
of mine own. All
          only
mine own. I say
          in all humility:
It is from me
          whence you derive
your English poetry."

"And what of your friends,

burnt at the stake?" I ask. "What
of Saunders, martyred
at St. Albans, for
preaching against
the Roman Church? He handed you
the cup of martyrdom..."

"He asked me would I
drain it? Would I die
with him
on the morrow?"

"You refused the cup..."

"No, I took it, as
he insisted, and I drank
instead
to his very good
health."

"And you were arrested, sentenced
to drawing-
and-quartering, then to
hanging..."

"They wanted
Ridley. I obliged, offering
everything I knew,

becking and bowing
my knee unto
Baal. And he had
his martyrdom, as
he wished it. And
I had my liberty."

"It's bastards," I say,
disgusted. "Bastards
that maketh
martyrs."

He studies me, accusing eye.
Then quoth: "If
I'm to be the bastard
        well Amen! Amen!
The bastards mayhap
        maketh martyrs,
but it's bastards still
that maketh
art."

So saying, pushing past me,
"Move, Bitch."

Then I lay broade awaking.

[Curtain]

Sandy McIntosh was born in Rockville Centre, New York, and received a BA from Southampton College, an MFA from Columbia University and a PhD. from the Union Graduate School. After working with children for eight years as a writer in the schools of Long Island's East End, Nassau County and in Brooklyn, he completed a study of writers who taught in the program and how their work with children affected their own writing. The study, *The Poets in the Poets-in-the Schools* was published by the University of Minnesota. For fifteen years he taught creative writing at Long Island University and Hofstra University while publishing nonfiction works, such as *Firing Back* (John Wiley & Sons), and computer software, such as *Mavis Beacon Teaches Typing!* (Electronic Arts). He has contributed journalism, poetry, and opinion columns to *The New York Times, Newsday, The Nation, The Wall Street Journal, The Long Island Press, American Book Review, The Daily Beast, PBS FRONTLINE* and elsewhere. He was also editor and publisher of *Wok Talk*, a Chinese cooking bi-monthly and the author and editor of several Chinese cook books and one of the first computer software cooking programs.

His first collection of poetry, *Earth Works,* was published by Southampton College in 1970, the year he graduated. He has since published six poetry collections: *Which Way to the Egress?* (1974), *Endless Staircase* (1994), *Between Earth and Sky* (2002), *The After-Death History of My Mother* (2005), *Forty-Nine Guaranteed Ways to Escape Death* (2007), *Ernesta, in the Style of the Flamenco* (2010) and also a collaboration with the poet Denise Duhamel, *237 More Reasons to Have Sex* (2009), *Cemetery Chess: Selected and New Poems* (2012). His memoir, *A Hole In the Ocean: A Hamptons' Apprenticeship* was published in 2016.

His original poetry in a screenplay won the Silver Medal in the Film Festival of the Americas. An excerpt from his collaboration with Denise Duhamel appears in *The Best American Poetry.*

He was Managing Editor of Long Island University's national literary journal, *Confrontation.* For more than a decade he was a host of Riverhead Cablevision's TV series, "Ideas and Images." Between 1990 and 2000, he was Chairman of the Distinguished Poet Series at Guild Hall, East Hampton. He was editor/publisher of *Survivor's Manual* magazine and books. He is currently publisher of Marsh Hawk Press.

Jane Augustine, *KRAZY: Visual Poems and Performance Scripts, A Woman's Guide to Mountain Climbing, Night Lights, Arbor Vitae*

Tom Beckett, ~~DIPSTICK~~ *(DIPTYCH)*

Sigman Byrd, *Under the Wanderer's Star*

Patricia Carlin, *Quantum Jitters, Original Green, Second Nature*

Claudia Carlson, *Pocket Park, The Elephant House, My Chocolate Sarcophagus*

Meredith Cole, *Miniatures*

Jon Curley, *Hybrid Moments*

Neil de la Flor, *An Elephant's Memory of Blizzards, Almost Dorothy*

Chard deNiord, *Sharp Golden Thorn*

Sharon Dolin, *Serious Pink*

Steve Fellner, *The Weary World Rejoices, Blind Date with Cavafy*

Thomas Fink, *Selected Poems & Poetic Series, Joyride, Peace Conference, Clarity and Other Poems, After Taxes, Gossip: A Book of Poems*

Norman Finkelstein, *Inside the Ghost Factory, Passing Over*

Edward Foster, *Sewing the Wind, Dire Straits, The Beginning of Sorrows, What He Ought To Know, Mahrem: Things Men Should Do for Men*

Robert Gibb, *After*

Paolo Javier, *The Feeling Is Actual*

Burt Kimmelman, *Somehow, Abandoned Angel*

Burt Kimmelman and Fred Caruso, *The Pond at Cape May Point*

Basil King, *The Spoken Word / the Painted Hand from Learning to Draw / A History 77 Beasts: Basil King's Bestiary, Mirage*

Martha King, *Imperfect Fit*

Phillip Lopate, *At the End of the Day: Selected Poems and An Introductory Essay*

Mary Mackey, *Travelers With No Ticket Home, Sugar Zone, Breaking the Fever*

Jason McCall, *Dear Hero,*

Sandy McIntosh, *A Hole In the Ocean: A Hamptons' Apprenticeship, Cemetery Chess: Selected and New Poems, Ernesta, in the Style of the Flamenco, Forty-Nine Guaranteed Ways to Escape Death, The After-Death History of My Mother, Between Earth and Sky*

Stephen Paul Miller, *Any Lie You Tell Will Be the Truth, There's Only One God and You're Not It, Fort Dad, The Bee Flies in May, Skinny Eighth Avenue*

Daniel Morris, *If Not for the Courage, Bryce Passage, Hit Play*

Sharon Olinka, *The Good City*

Christina Olivares, *No Map of the Earth Includes Stars*

Justin Petropoulos, *Eminent Domain*

Paul Pines, *Divine Madness, Last Call at the Tin Palace, Charlotte Songs*

Jacquelyn Pope, *Watermark*

George Quasha, *Things Done For Themselves*

Karin Randolph, *Either She Was*

Rochelle Ratner, *Ben Casey Days, Balancing Acts, House and Home*

Michael Rerick, *In Ways Impossible to Fold*

Corrine Robins, *Facing It: New and Selected Poems, Today's Menu, One Thousand Years*

Eileen R. Tabios, *The Connoisseur of Alleys, Sun Stigmata, The Thorn Rosary: Selected Prose Poems and New (1998–2010), The Light Sang As It Left Your Eyes: Our Autobiography, I Take Thee, English, for My Beloved, Reproductions of the Empty Flagpole*

Eileen R. Tabios and j/j hastain, *the relational elatiqns of ORPHANED ALGEBRA*

Susan Terris, *Ghost of Yesterday, Natural Defenses*

Madeline Tiger, *Birds of Sorrow and Joy*

Tana Jean Welch, *Latest Volcano*

Harriet Zinnes, *New and Selected Poems, Weather Is Whether, Light Light or the Curvature of the Earth, Whither Nonstopping, Drawing on the Wall*

YEAR	AUTHOR	MHP POETRY PRIZE TITLE	JUDGE
2004	Jacquelyn Pope	Watermark	Marie Ponsot
2005	Sigman Byrd	Under the Wanderer's Star	Gerald Stern
2006	Steve Fellner	Blind Date With Cavafy	Denise Duhamel
2007	Karin Randolph	Either She Was	David Shapiro
2008	Michael Rerick	In Ways Impossible to Fold	Thylias Moss
2009	Neil de la Flor	Almost Dorothy	Forrest Gander
2010	Justin Petropoulos	Eminent Domain	Anne Waldman
2011	Meredith Cole	Miniatures	Alicia Ostriker
2012	Jason McCall	Dear Hero,	Cornelius Eady
2013	Tom Beckett	~~DIPSTICK~~ (DIPTYCH)	Charles Bernstein
2014	Christina Olivares	No Map of the Earth Includes Stars	Brenda Hillman
2015	Tana Jean Welch	Latest Volcano	Stephanie Strickland
2016	Robert Gibb	After	Mark Doty

For more information, please go to: www.marshhawkpress.org